Getting to k...

Classical or Spanish guitar

This type of guitar has nylon strings which give a mellow sound and are easy to press down. These guitars are available in various sizes to suit the size of your hands.

Parts of the guitar

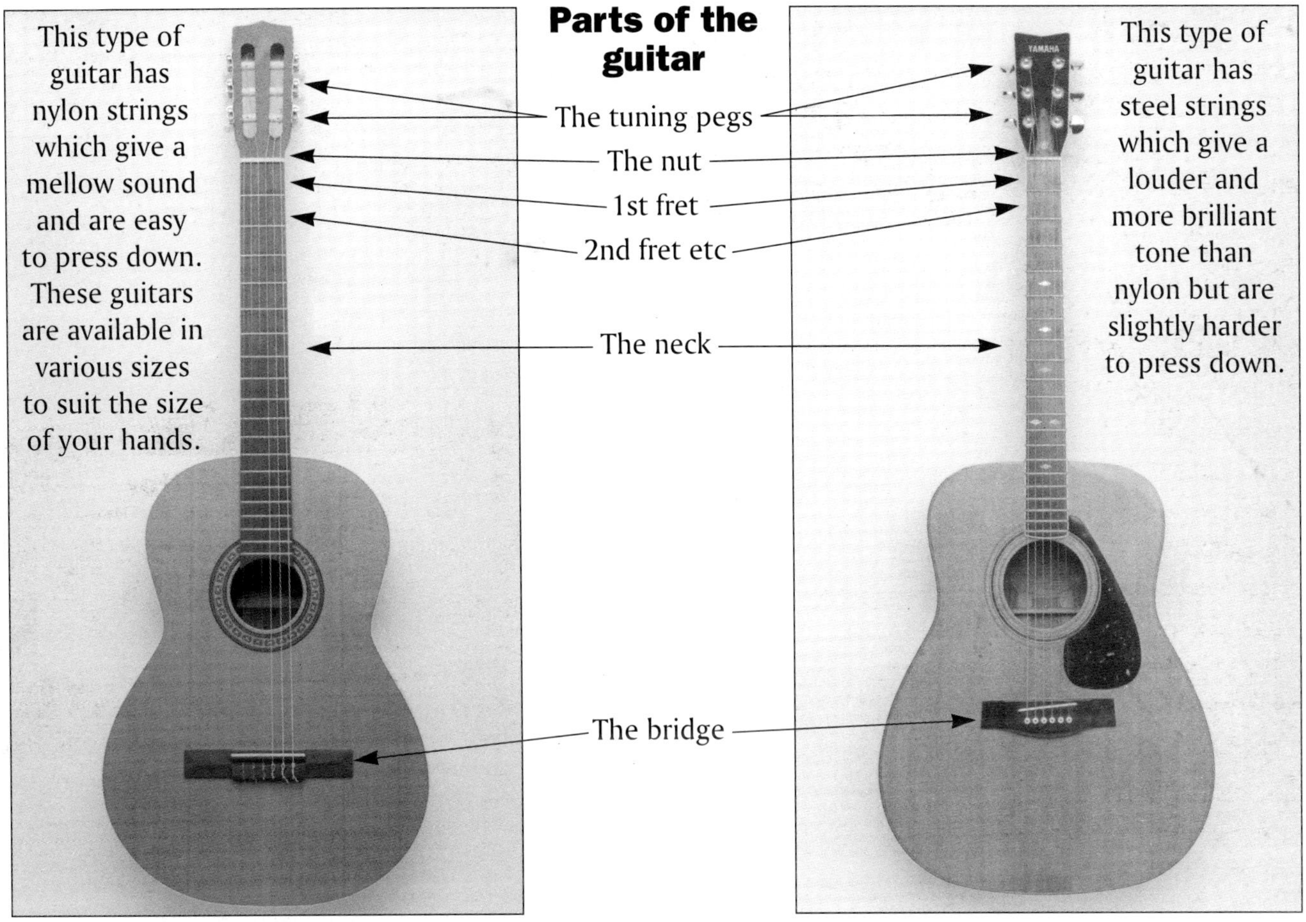

- The tuning pegs
- The nut
- 1st fret
- 2nd fret etc
- The neck
- The bridge

Flat top or jumbo guitar

This type of guitar has steel strings which give a louder and more brilliant tone than nylon but are slightly harder to press down.

How to hold the guitar

Pick Up The Guitar © Peter Flanagan & Dave Mallinson Publications 1997

How to tune your guitar

Method 1
- tuning to a keyboard

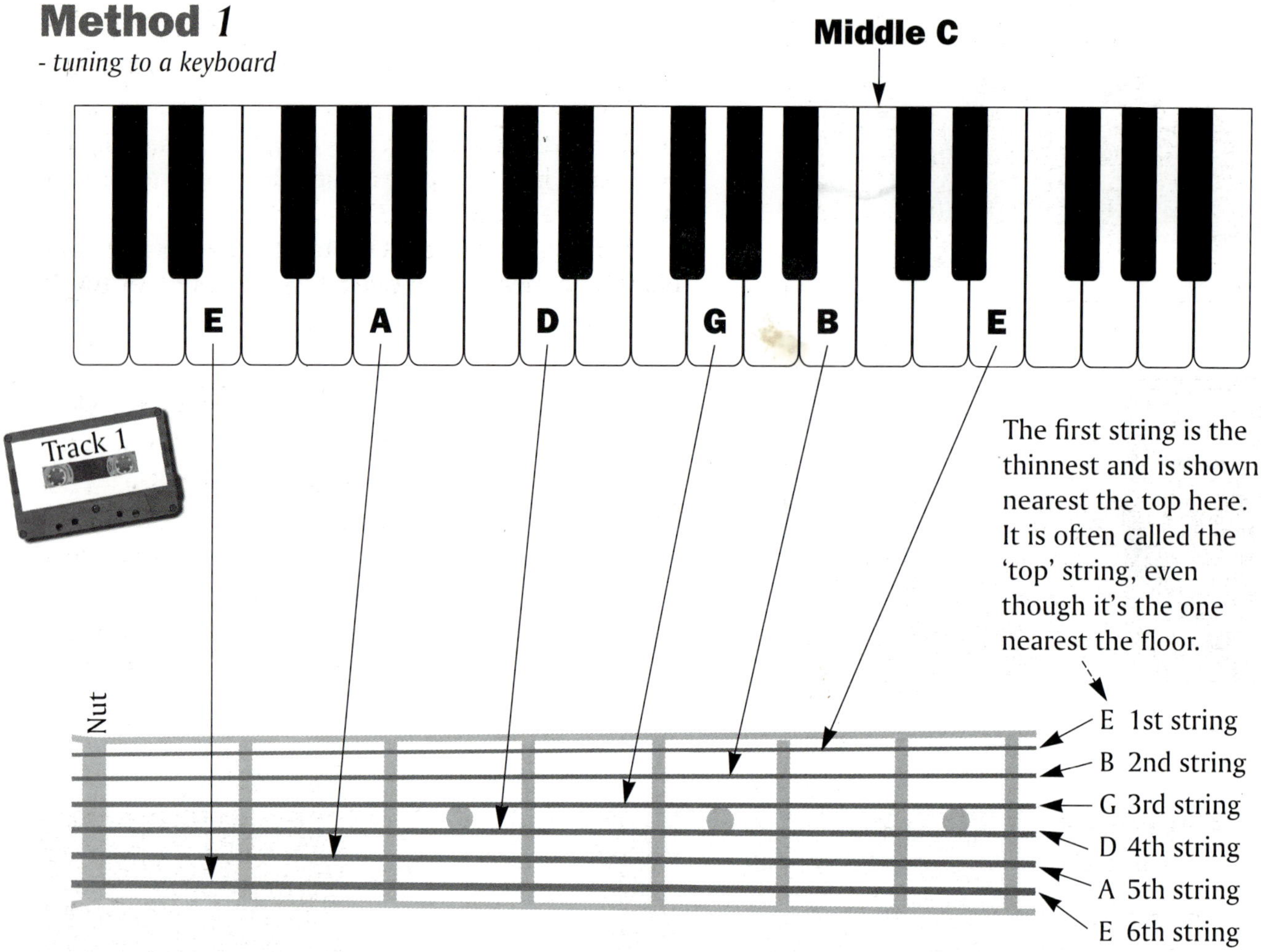

Middle C

Track 1

The first string is the thinnest and is shown nearest the top here. It is often called the 'top' string, even though it's the one nearest the floor.

E 1st string
B 2nd string
G 3rd string
D 4th string
A 5th string
E 6th string

Method 2
- tuning to the guitar itself

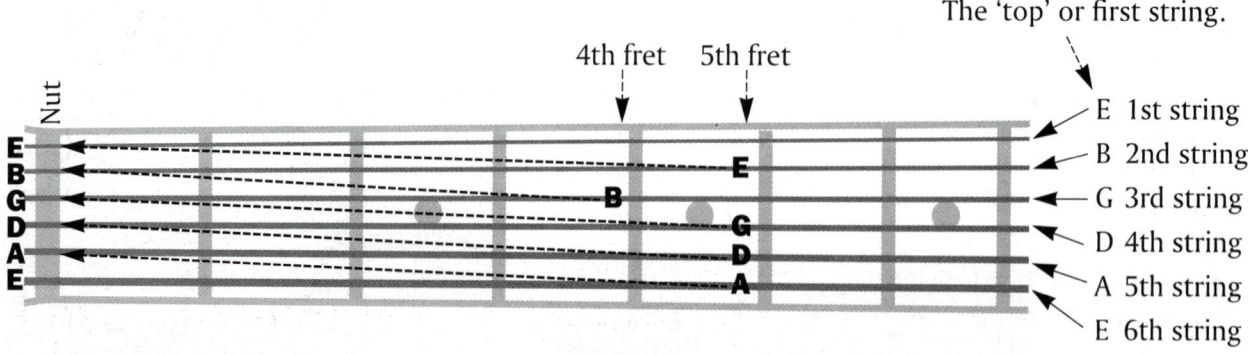

The 'top' or first string.

4th fret   5th fret

E 1st string
B 2nd string
G 3rd string
D 4th string
A 5th string
E 6th string

To use **Method 2** at least one of your strings should be at the correct pitch or as near as you can get it, then you can tune the other strings to it.

The 6th string fretted at the 5th fret = the 5th string open
The 5th string fretted at the 5th fret = the 4th string open
The 4th string fretted at the 5th fret = the 3rd string open
The 3rd string fretted at the 4th fret = the 2nd string open
The 2nd string fretted at the 5th fret = the 1st string open

Pick Up The Guitar © Peter Flanagan & Dave Mallinson Publications 1997

Tuning up and replacing strings

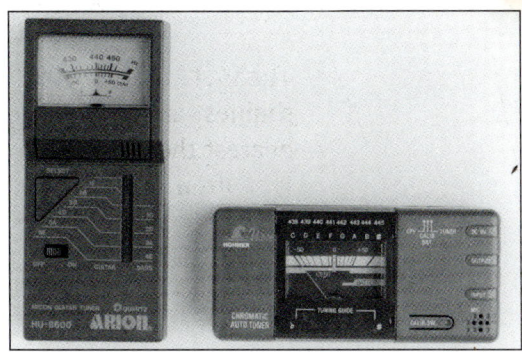

Method 3
-pitch pipes

Shown here is a set of pitch pipes, with one pipe for each string of the guitar: Low E, A, D, G, B and High E. Blow *gently* into each pipe in turn. Blowing too hard can put the pipe out of tune. Pipes work well with **Method 2**. Try this: tune your 6th string to the Low E on the pipes (or as near as you can get it) then use **Method** 2.

Method 4
- electronic tuners

At first, you'll probably find it very difficult if not impossible to tune up without help. If this is the case, an electronic tuner will solve your problem.

Tuners can be expensive but can change some peoples' lives. Remember, if you want to play *you've got to get in tune*.

Replacing strings

Leave plenty of slack to wind around the tuning pegs, especially on the thinner strings. This will stop them slipping.

New strings (especially nylon) will stretch at first. Just keep re-tuning them until they settle down. At this stage you can nip off the string ends, leaving a couple of centimetres.

Nylon

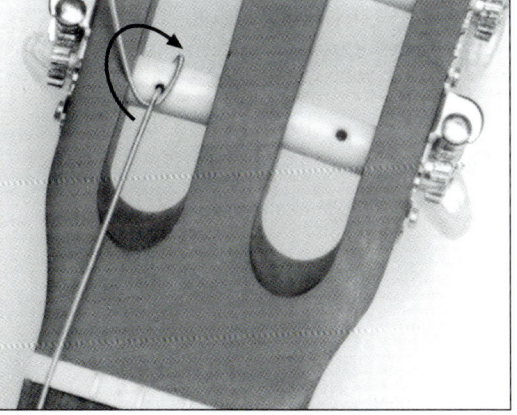

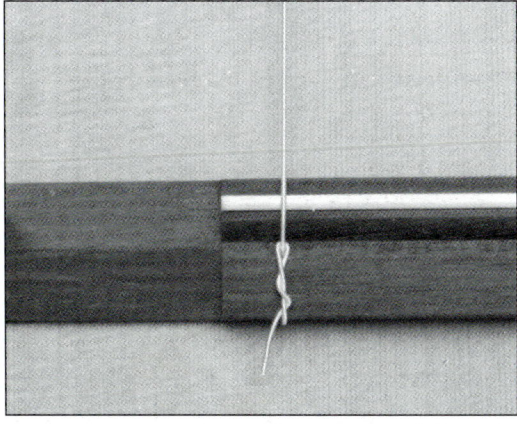

Old strings of any material sound dull and are hard to tune. Don't mix old and new strings. If in doubt, replace the whole set.

Steel

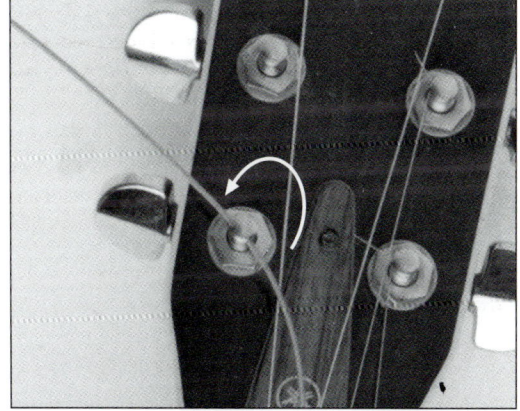

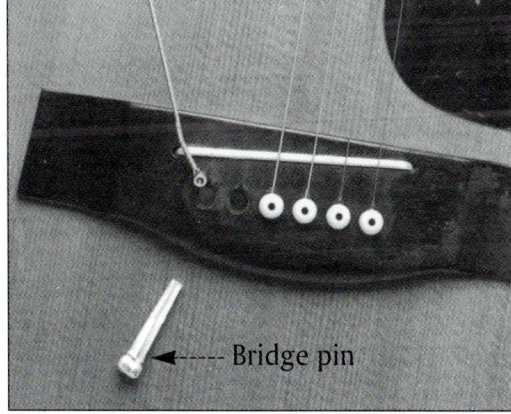

←----- Bridge pin

Steel strings will last longer if you wipe them with a cloth on top and underneath after each use.

Pick Up The Guitar © Peter Flanagan & Dave Mallinson Publications 1997

4 The left hand

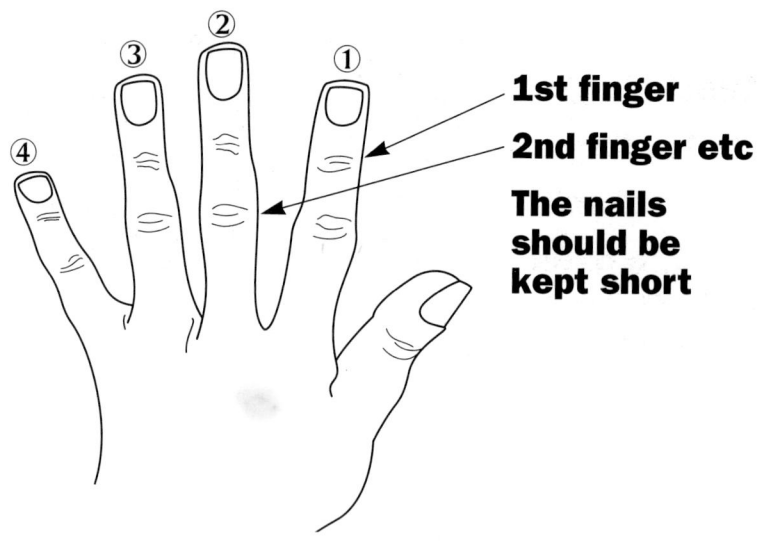

1st finger
2nd finger etc
The nails should be kept short

D7

Fretting a D7 chord

To produce a clear sound, the fingers should be close behind the fret wires and not touching neighbouring strings. They should press the strings against the fingerboard just firmly enough that the strings don't buzz when strummed.

D7

3 easy chords to practise

Note:
x means *don't* play that string
o means open (unfretted) string

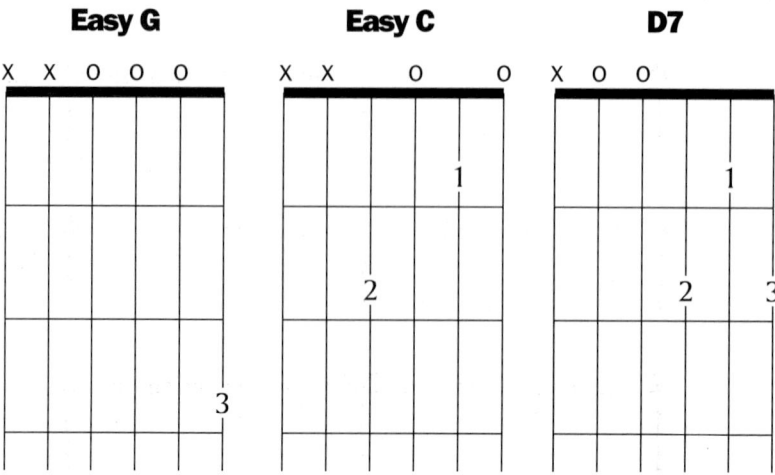

Easy G   Easy C   D7

Pick Up The Guitar © Peter Flanagan & Dave Mallinson Publications 1997

The right hand   5

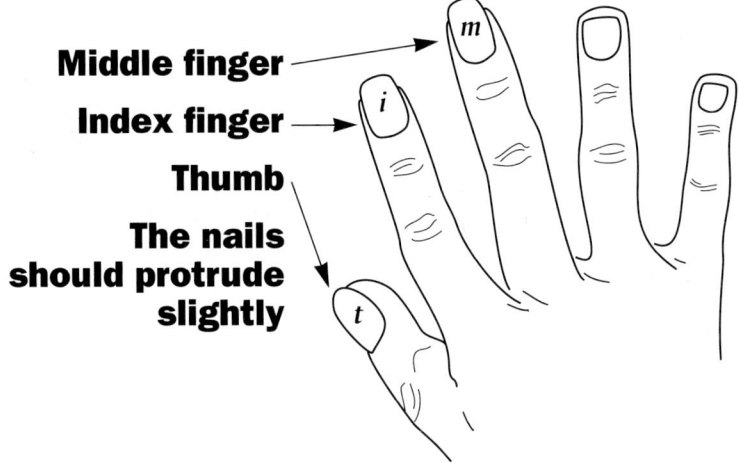

- Middle finger → *m*
- Index finger → *i*
- Thumb
- The nails should protrude slightly → *t*

Easy strum

Use your thumb to strum down across the first four strings and try the chords to *Coming Round the Mountain*.
Each stroke / represents one strum. Change chord where marked.

Track 2

G Com - ing round the   moun - tain when she   comes,
| / / / / | / / / / | / / / / | / / / / |

Count: 1   2   3   4   1   2   3   4   etc.

G Com - ing round the   moun - tain when she **D7** comes,
| / / / / | / / / / | / / / / | / / / / |

G Com - ing round the   moun - tain,   **C** Com - ing round the   moun - tain,
| / / / / | / / / / | / / / / | / / / / |

G Com - ing round the **D7** moun - tain when she **G** comes.
| / / / / | / / / / | / / / / | / / / / |

Pick Up The Guitar © Peter Flanagan & Dave Mallinson Publications 1997

6 Reading tablature

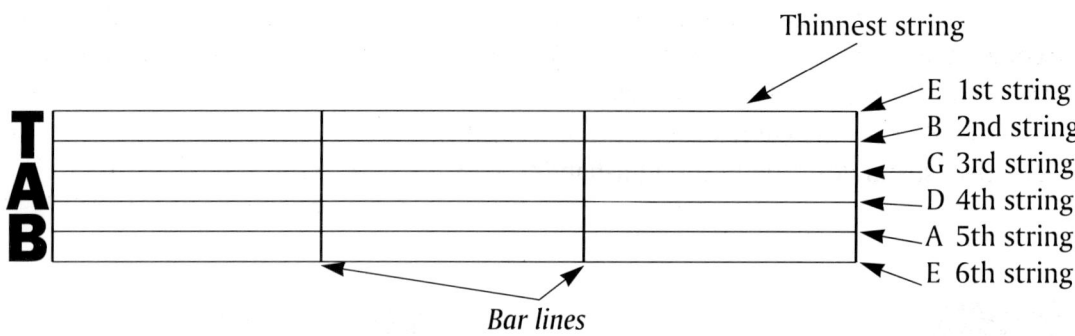

The six lines shown to the right represent the six strings of the guitar. These six lines (collectively a *stave*) are divided into equal measures with *bar lines*.

On these lines are written the number of the fret to be played (pressed down with a finger of your left hand), in this case close behind the *3rd* fret on the *6th* (thickest) string.

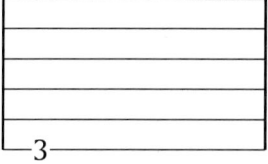

If a string is marked with a zero, that means the string is played *open,* that is, don't press it down with your left hand.

Now try the scale of *G major:*

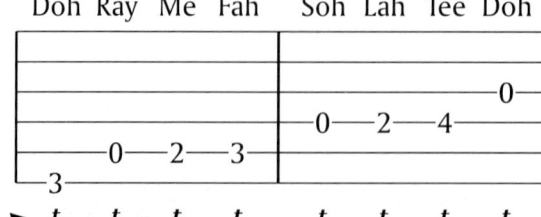

Pluck **down** with your thumb.

When notes are placed over each other, strum down evenly (from the thickest, or lowest, string to the top, or thinnest) with your thumb.

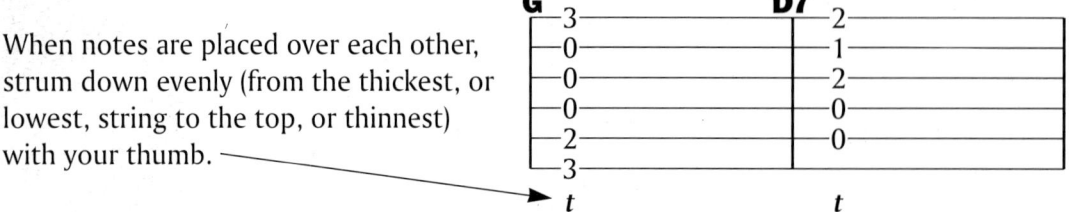

Pick Up The Guitar © Peter Flanagan & Dave Mallinson Publications 1997

More left hand information & chords   7

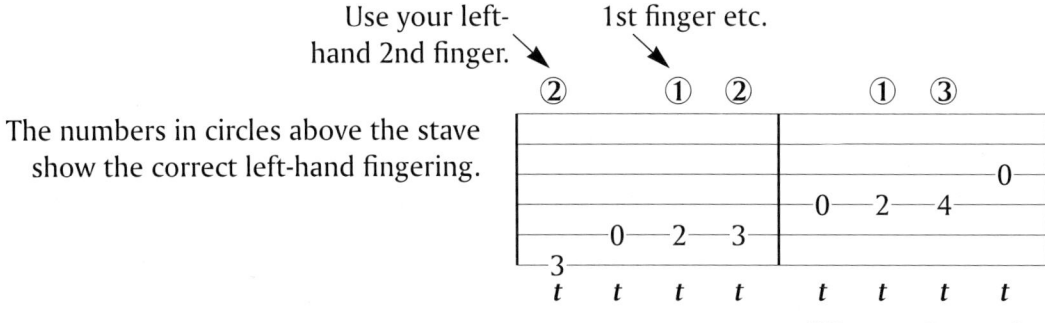

Use your left-hand 2nd finger.

1st finger etc.

The numbers in circles above the stave show the correct left-hand fingering.

The chords

The chords above the stave are shown for accompaniment by a guitar or banjo etc. You won't always be fretting a chord when playing the tunes.

Following are the chords used in this book. To practise, strum down with the right-hand thumb.

If you hear any muffled strings, check that your fingers are close behind (but not touching) the fretwire. Also, make sure they're not damping neighbouring strings. When you can fret the chords cleanly, try slowly changing from one to another, gradually building up speed as you practise.

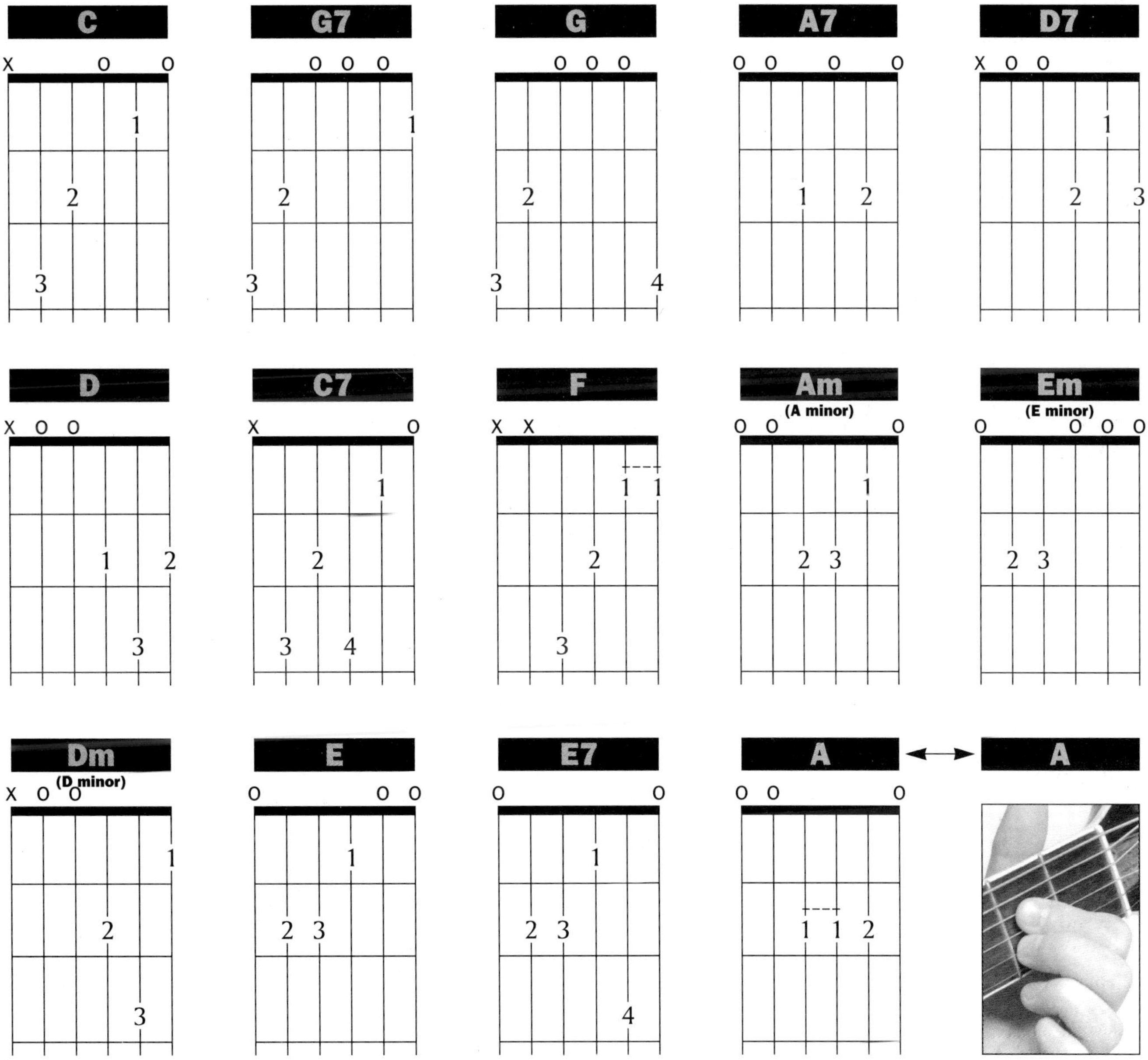

Pick Up The Guitar © Peter Flanagan & Dave Mallinson Publications 1997

The basic right-hand strum

Fingerstyle

Step 1

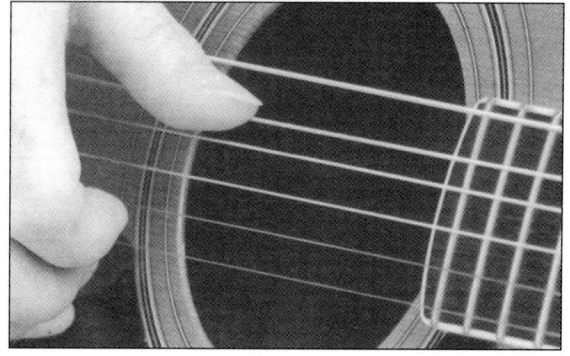

Track 3

Keep the hand relaxed

Step 2

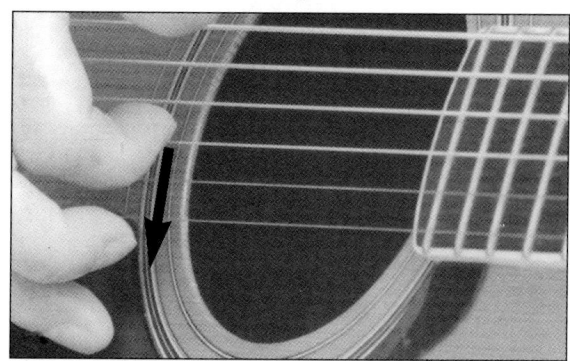

Firstly, fret a chord of C (see previous page). Then, with the *thumb,* pluck *down* on one of the lower (bass) strings for the 1st beat.

Next, using the back of your nail, strum *down* with the index finger across the first three treble strings for the 2nd beat.

It sounds like this:

Boom ——————————————————— *Chick*

Or: 1 ——————————————————— 2

Plectrum style

Step 1

Keep the hand relaxed

Step 2

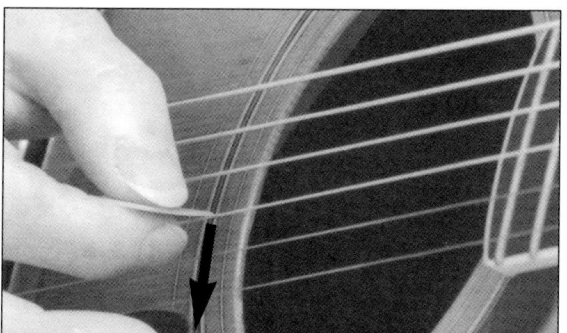

First, fret a chord of C (see previous page), then angle the plectrum as shown and pluck *down* on one of the lower (bass) strings for the 1st beat.

Next, with a twist of your wrist angle the plectrum as shown and strum *down* across the first three treble strings for the 2nd beat.

It sounds like this: *Boom* ——————— *Chick*

Or: 1 ——————— 2

Plectrums

Plectrums are available in many shapes and sizes but are inexpensive. Try several until you find the type you're comfortable with. Note: plectrums are not normally used on nylon strings. Grip the plectrum firmly between the thumb and index finger, but not so tight as to cramp up your hand.

How to hold the plectrum

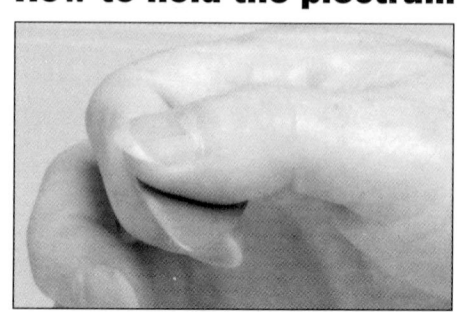

Pick Up The Guitar © Peter Flanagan & Dave Mallinson Publications 1997

How to play a tune

First - basic accompaniment

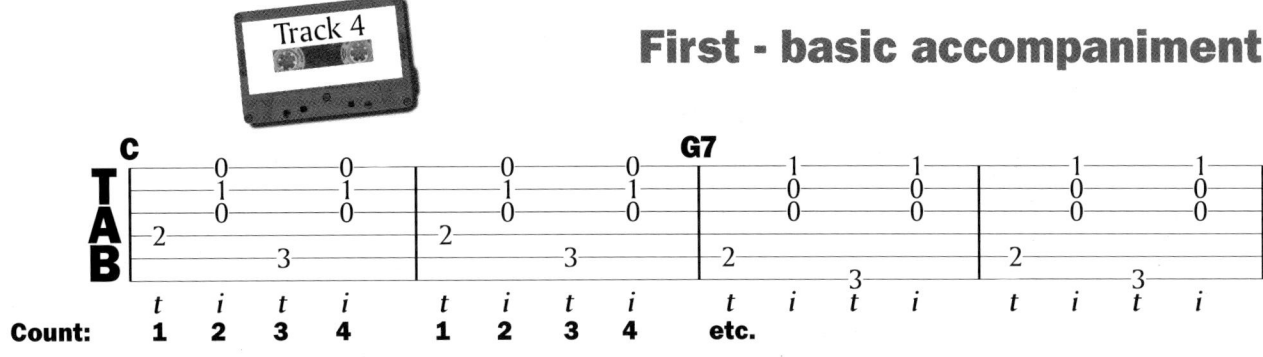

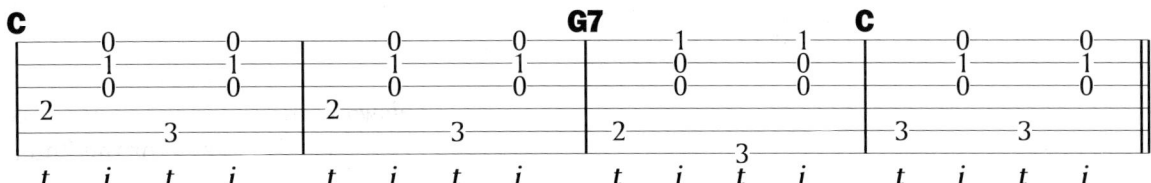

Fingerstyle:
t = pluck *down* with your thumb
i = strum *down* with your index finger.

Plectrum:
Pluck all notes *down* with the plectrum.

Next
- by selecting which string to play with your thumb or your plectrum, you can pick out a simple tune. Try *Skip to My Lou*.

Play all the notes clearly and play slowly but with an even beat.

Skip to My Lou

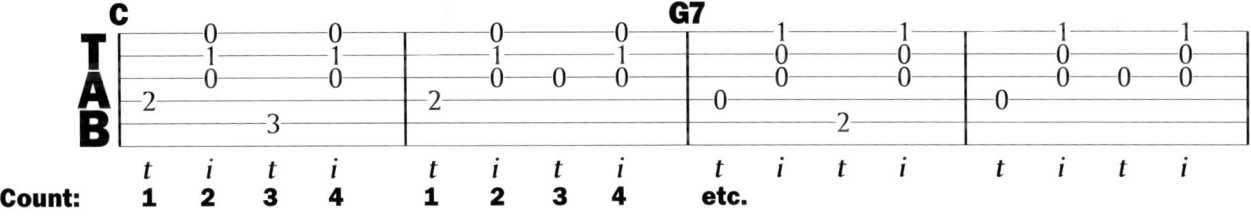

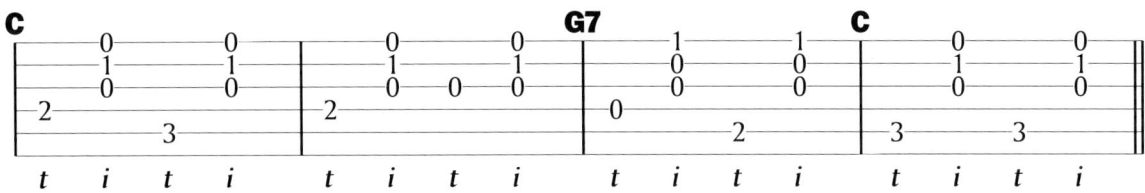

Pick Up The Guitar © Peter Flanagan & Dave Mallinson Publications 1997

Silver Threads Among the Gold

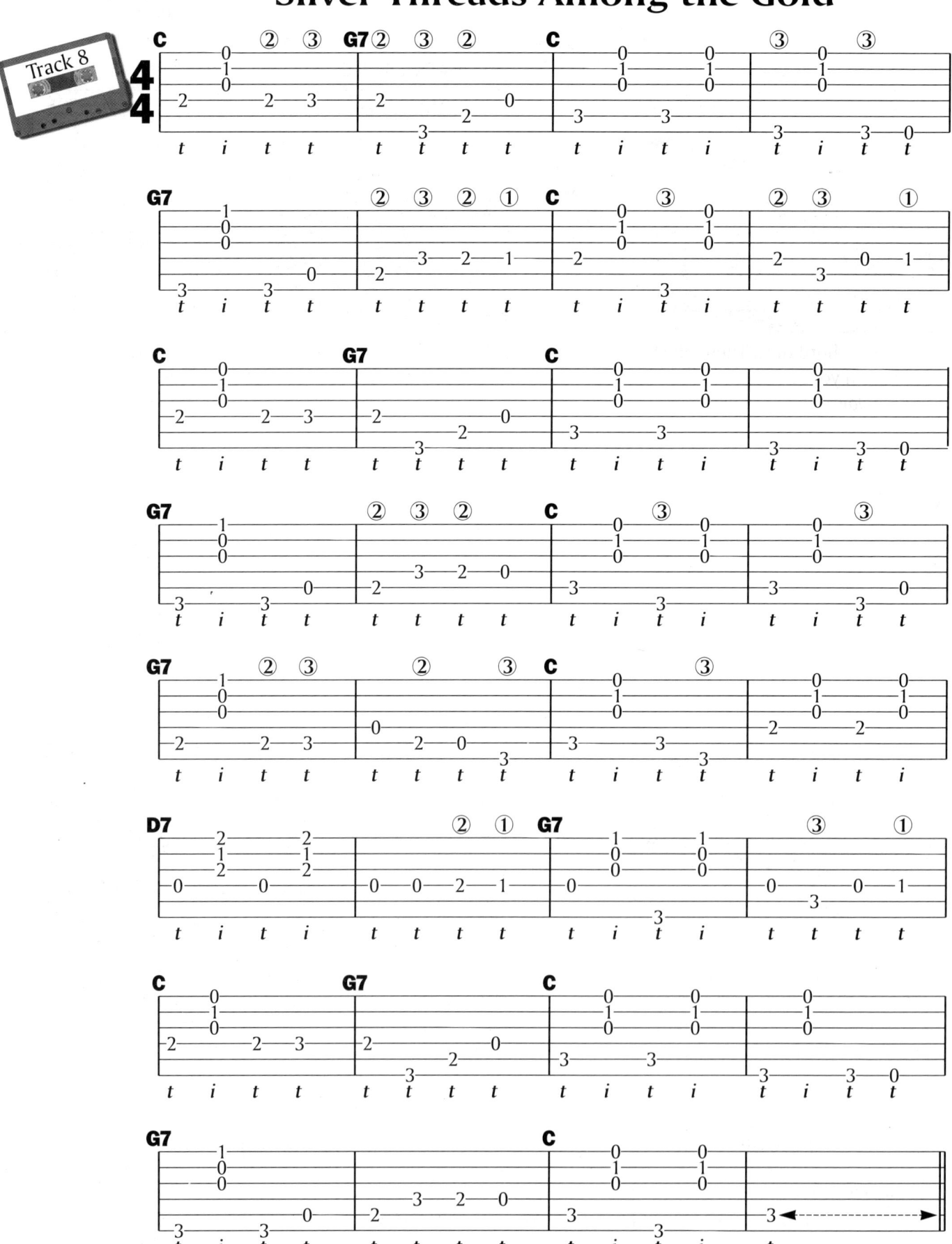

The double strum 13

Track 9

Fingerstyle

Step 1
Long note

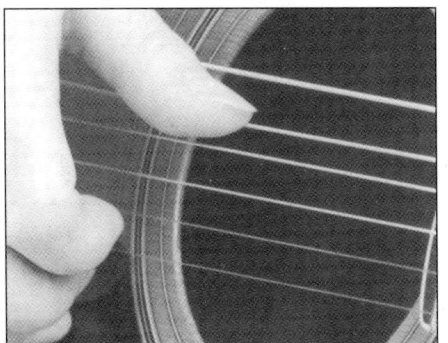

First, fret a chord of C. Then, pluck down with your *thumb* on one of the *lower* (bass) strings.

|— 1st beat —|

Step 2
Short note   **Short note**

Keep the hand relaxed

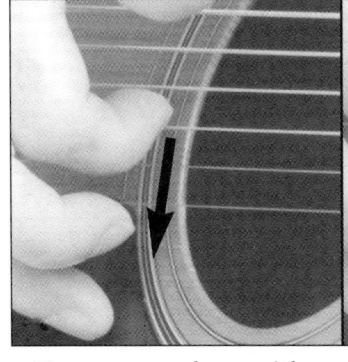 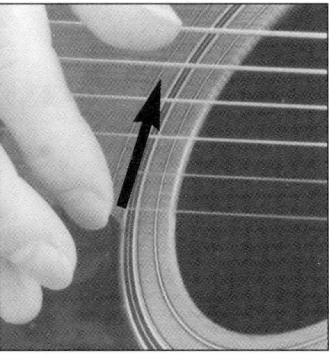

Next, strum *down* with the *index finger* across the *first three* (treble) strings.

Then, quickly strum back *up* with the *index finger* across the *first two* (treble) strings.

|————— 2nd beat —————|

It sounds like this:
      Boom ————————— *Chick* ————— *a*

Or: 1 ————————————— 2 ————— and

Plectrum style

Step 1
Long note

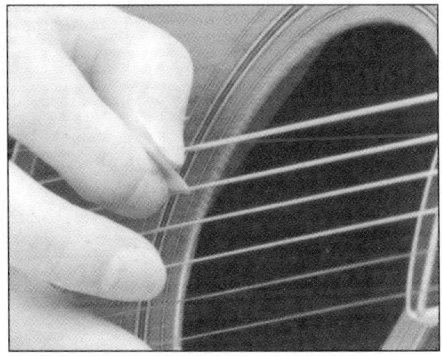

First, fret a chord of C and then angle the plectrum as shown; pluck *down* on one of the *lower* (bass) strings.

|— 1st beat —|

Step 2
Short note   **Short note**

Keep the hand relaxed

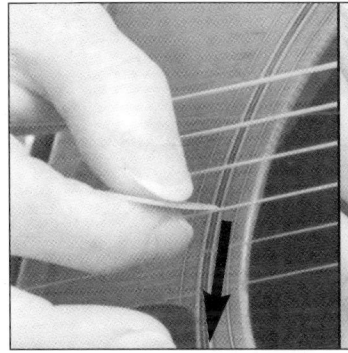 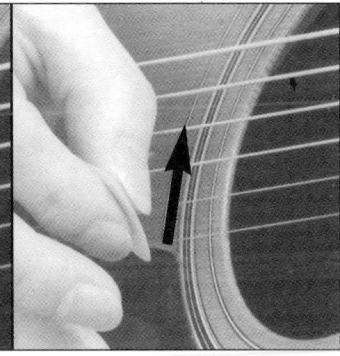

Next, with a twist of your wrist, angle the plectrum as shown and strum *down* across the *first three* treble strings.

Then, angle the plectrum as shown and quickly strum back *up* across the *first two* treble strings.

|————— 2nd beat —————|

It sounds like this:
      Boom ————————— *Chick* ————— *a*

Or: 1 ————————————— 2 ————— and

Pick Up The Guitar © Peter Flanagan & Dave Mallinson Publications 1997

14 Tunes using the double strum

Aunt Rhody

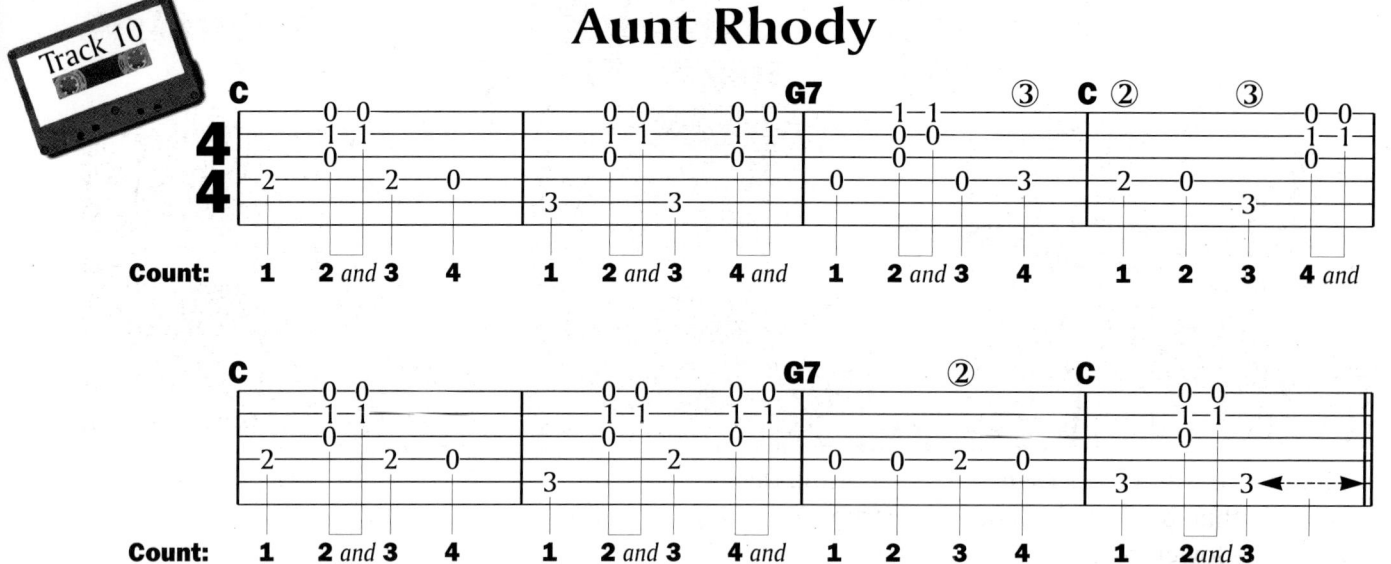

Michael, Row the Boat Ashore

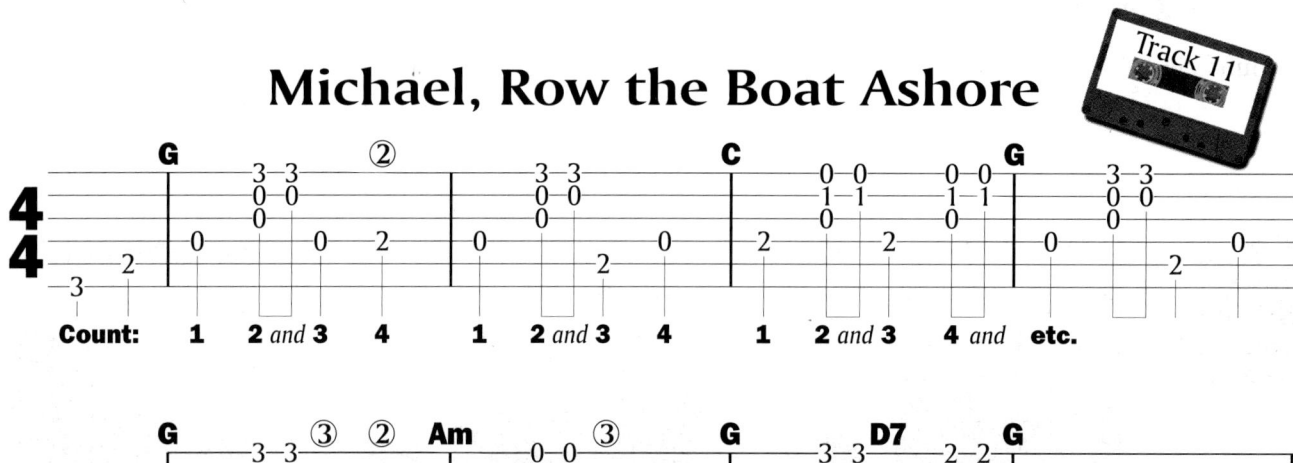

The Drunken Sailor

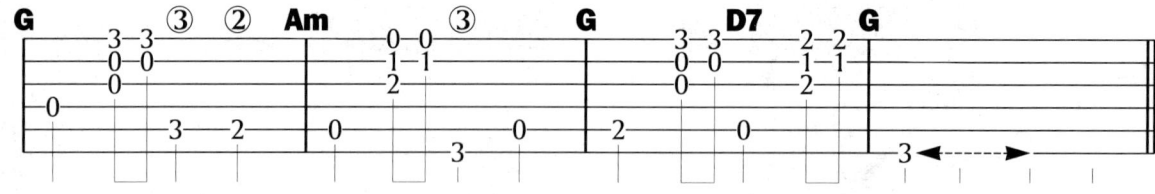
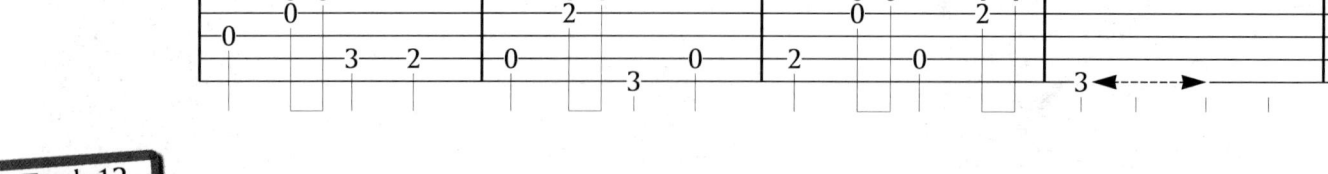
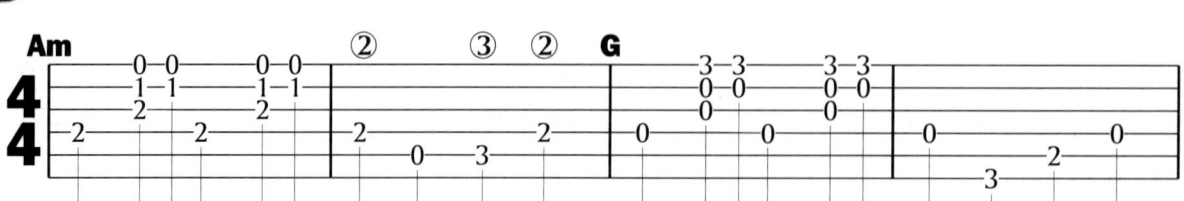
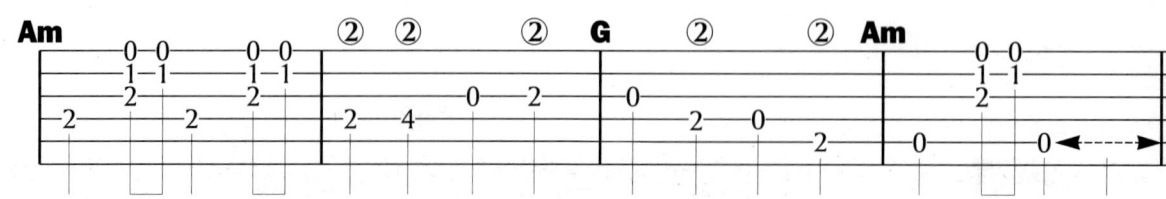

Pick Up The Guitar © Peter Flanagan & Dave Mallinson Publications 1997

The basic strum in waltz time 15

Keep the hand relaxed

Track 13

Fingerstyle

Step 1

First, fret a chord of C. Then, with your thumb, pluck *down* on one of the lower (bass) strings. **Put a strong accent on this beat.**

⎿──── **1st beat** ────⏌

Step 2

Next, using the back of your nail, strum *down* with your index finger across the first three treble strings.

⎿──── **2nd beat** ────⏌

Step 3

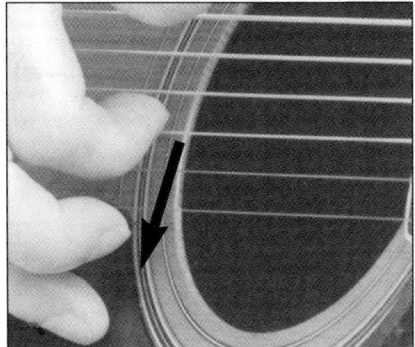

Then, strum *down* again with the index finger across the *same* first three treble strings.

⎿──── **3rd beat** ────⏌

It sounds like this:
　　　　Boom ─────────── *Chick* ─────────── *Chick*
Or:　　　1 ──────────────── 2 ──────────────── 3

Note: There should be a strong accent on the first beat.

Plectrum style

Step 1

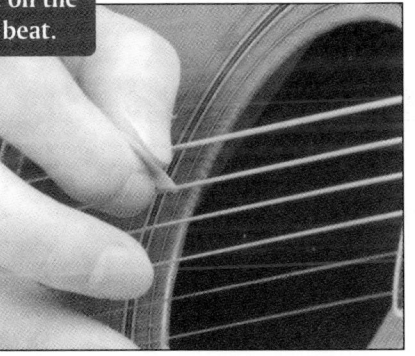

First, fret a chord of C. Then, angle the plectrum as shown and pluck *down* on one of the lower (bass) strings.

⎿──── **1st beat** ────⏌

Step 2

Next, with a twist of your wrist, angle the plectrum as shown and strum *down* across the first three treble strings.

⎿──── **2nd beat** ────⏌

Step 3

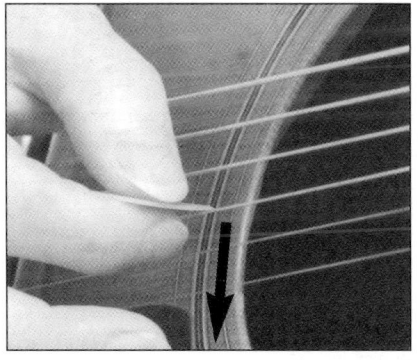

Then, keeping the plectrum at the same angle, strum *down* again across the same first three treble strings.

⎿──── **3rd beat** ────⏌

It sounds like this:
　　　　Boom ─────────── *Chick* ─────────── *Chick*
Or:　　　1 ──────────────── 2 ──────────────── 3

Put a strong accent on this beat.

Remember: **DO** play all three steps evenly.

▶ **Step 1 = 1st beat**　　**Step 2 = 2nd beat**　　**Step 3 = 3rd beat** ▶

Pick Up The Guitar © Peter Flanagan & Dave Mallinson Publications 1997

Tunes using the basic waltz-time strum

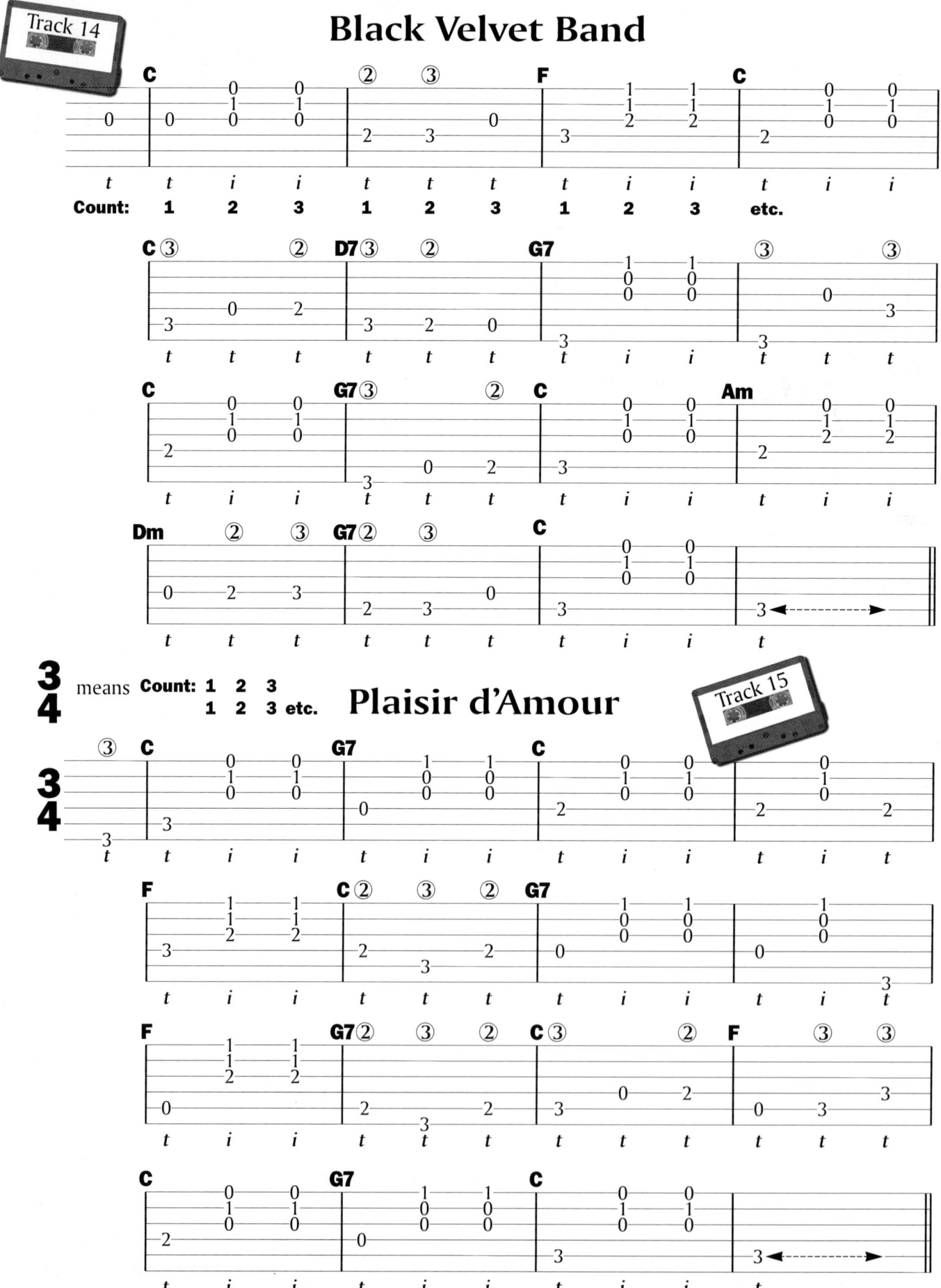

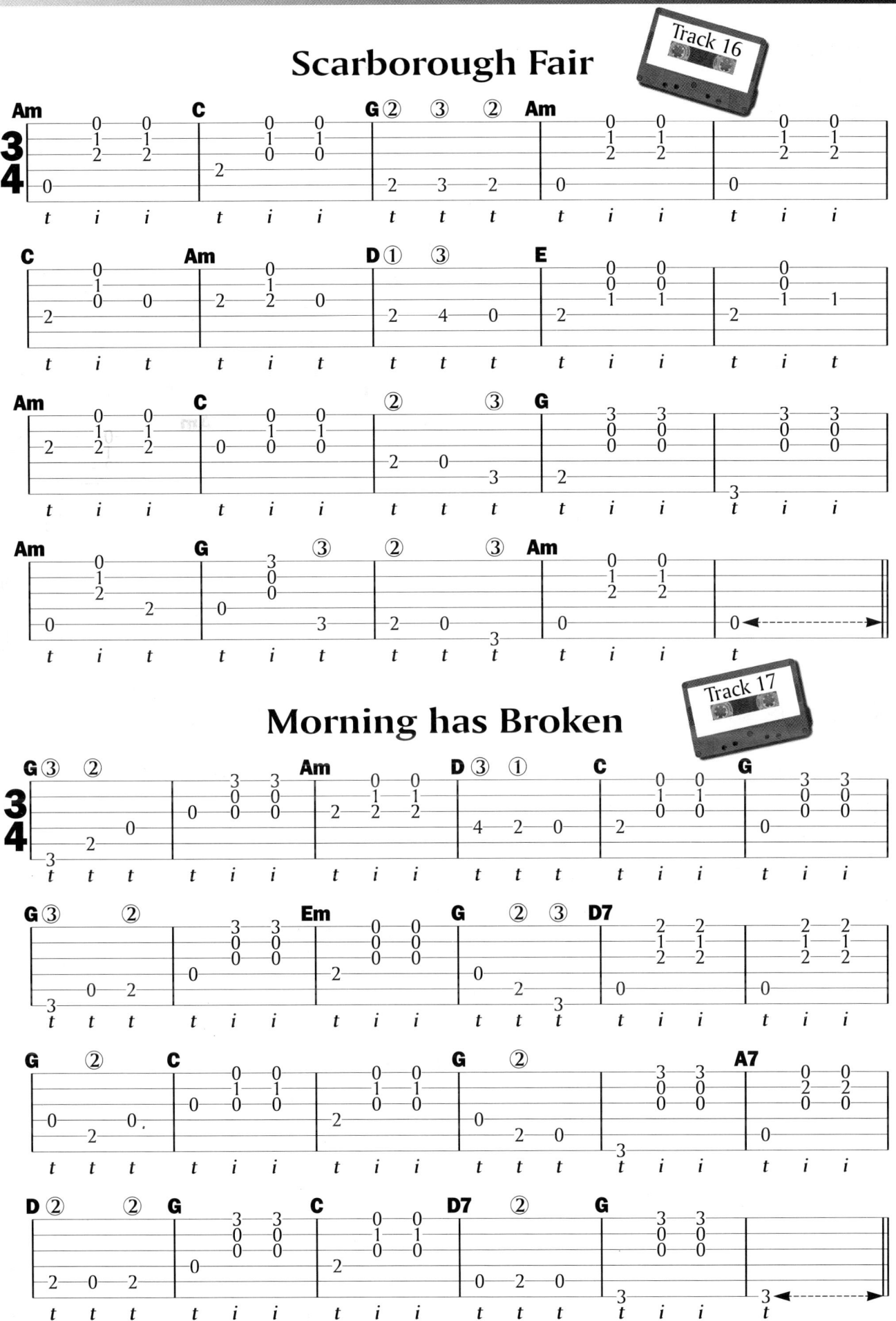

My Bonny

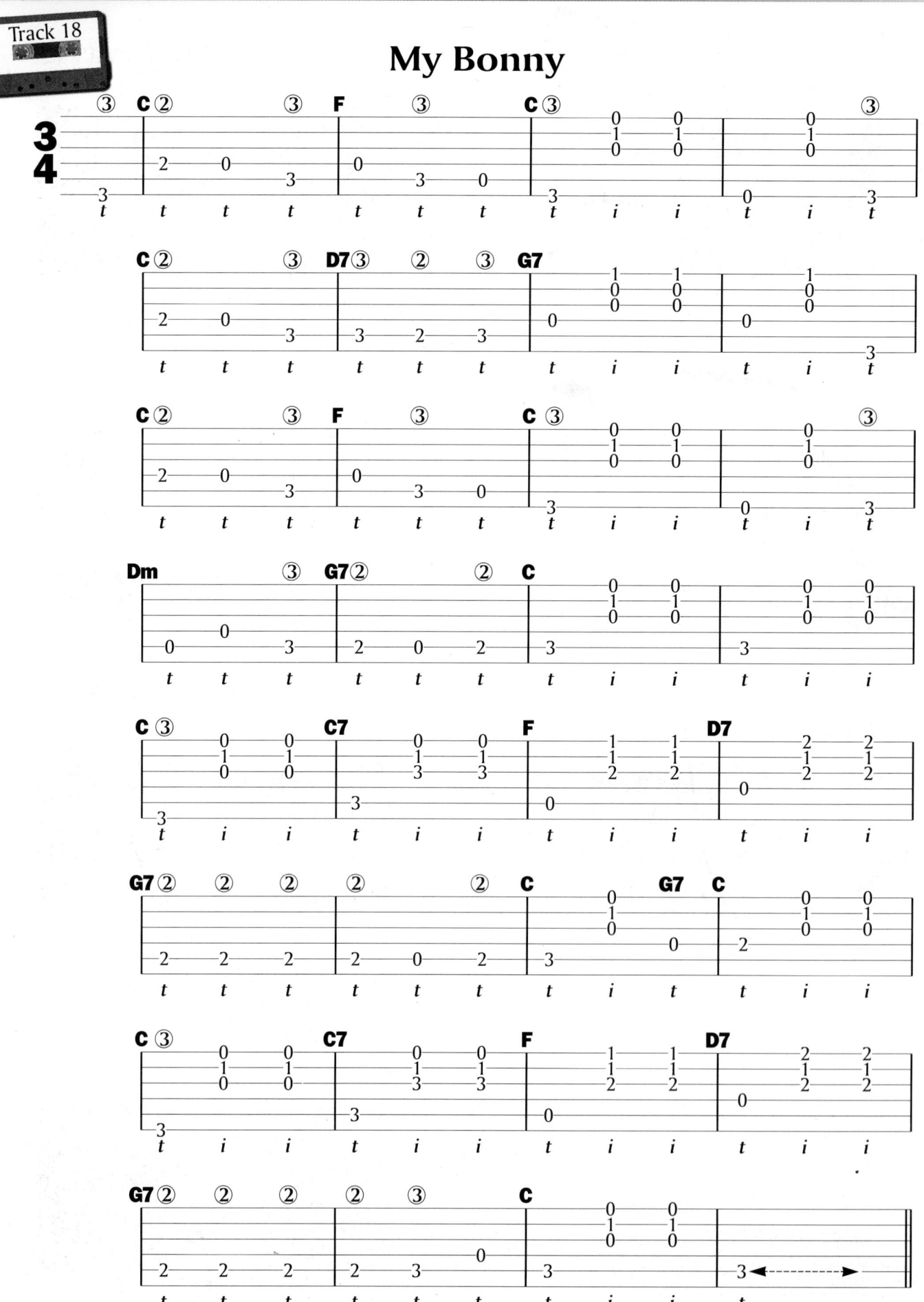

The double strum in waltz time 19

Track 19

Fingerstyle

Step 1 Long note

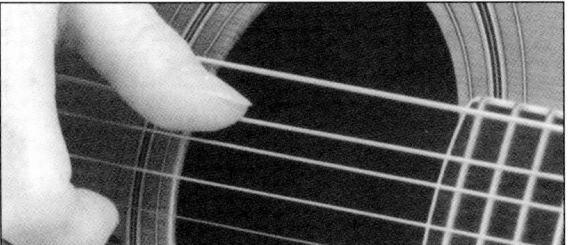

First fret a chord and pluck *down* on a bass string with your thumb.

— 1st beat —

Short Step 2 Short

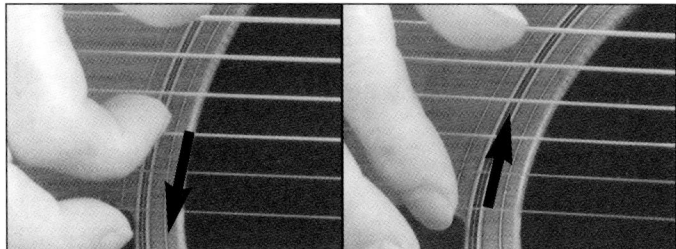

Next, strum *down* across the first 3 treble strings with the index finger and then *quickly* strum back up across the first *two* treble strings for the 2nd beat.

— 2nd beat —

Keep the hand relaxed

The whole strum should sound like this:

Boom Chick-a Chick-a
Or: *1   2 and   3 and*

Note: There should be a strong accent on the first beat.

Short Step 3 Short

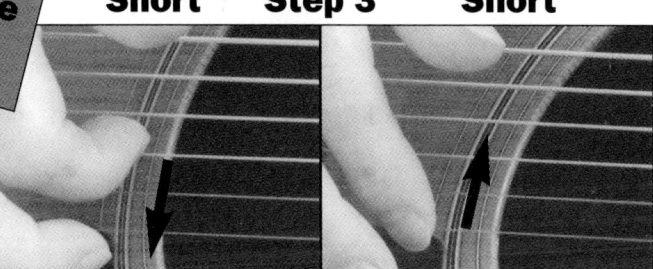

Lastly, repeat **Step 2** for the 3rd beat.

— 3rd beat —

Plectrum style

Step 1 Long note

First, fret a chord, angle the plectrum as shown and pluck down on a bass string.

— 1st beat —

Short Step 2 Short

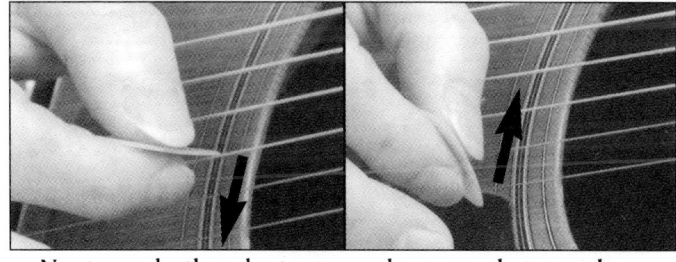

Next, angle the plectrum as shown and strum *down* across the first 3 treble strings. Then, angle the plectrum as shown and *quickly* strum back up across the first 2 treble strings.

— 2nd beat —

The whole strum should sound like this:

Boom Chick-a Chick-a
Or: *1   2 and   3 and*

Note: There should be a strong accent on the first beat.

Short Step 3 Short

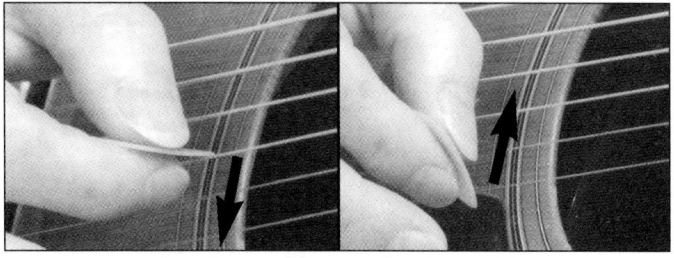

Lastly, repeat **Step 2** for the 3rd beat.

— 3rd beat —

Pick Up The Guitar © Peter Flanagan & Dave Mallinson Publications 1997

Tunes using the waltz time double strum

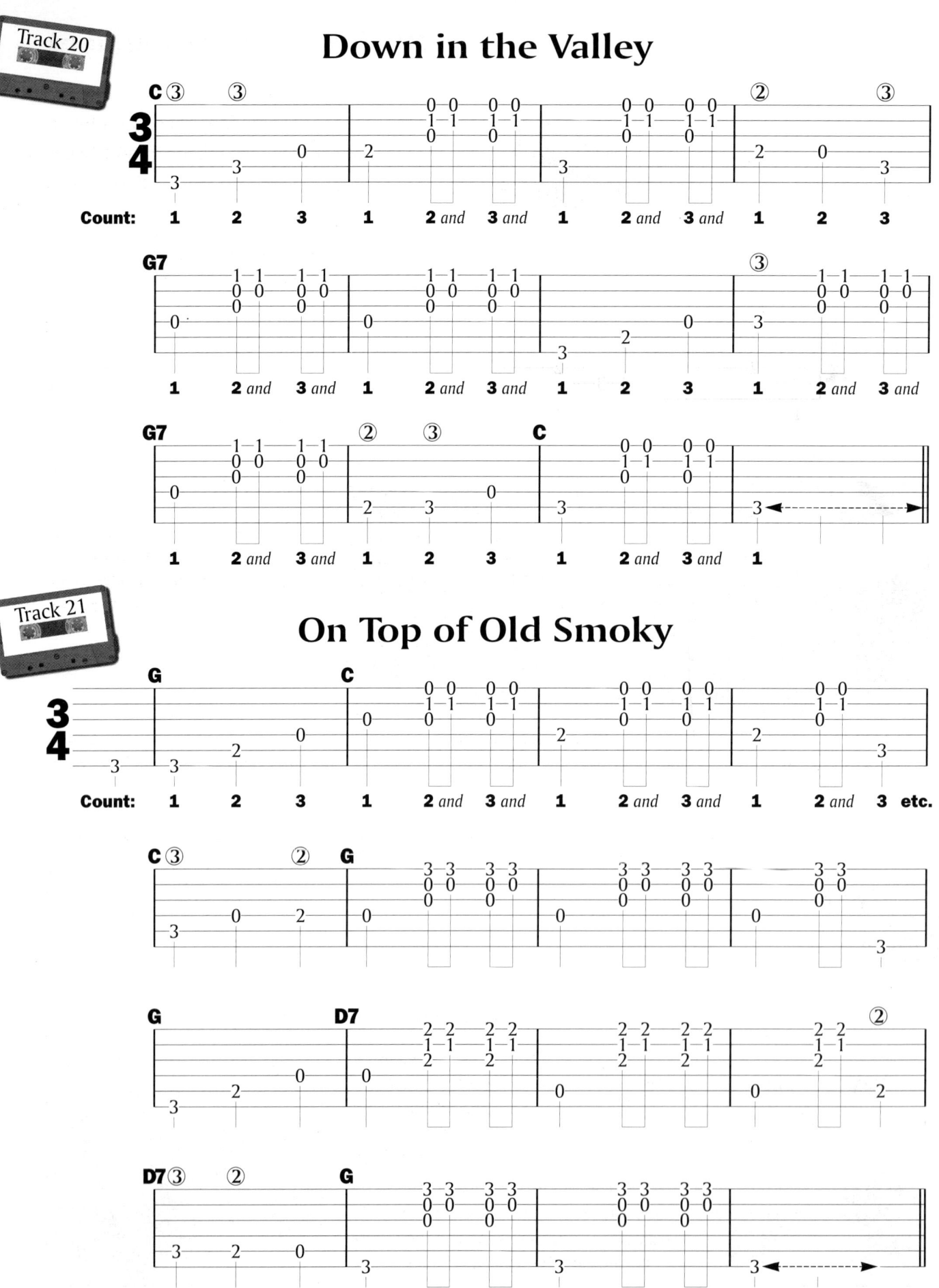

Fingerpicking

The bass accompaniment

t means the **right-hand thumb**
i means the **right-hand index finger**
m means the **right-hand middle finger**
(See page 5)

Using the right-hand thumb *(t)*, pluck down on the 5th and 4th string (in this case) alternately, *keeping an even beat.*

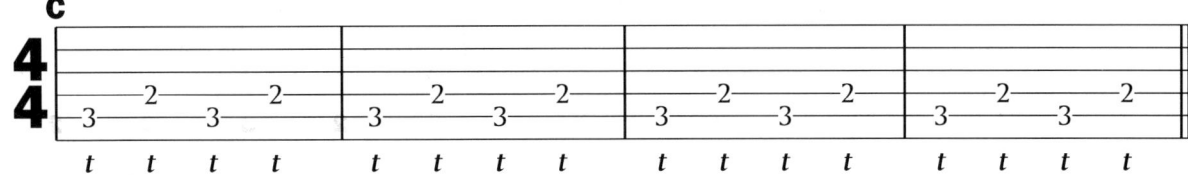

Picking the tunes

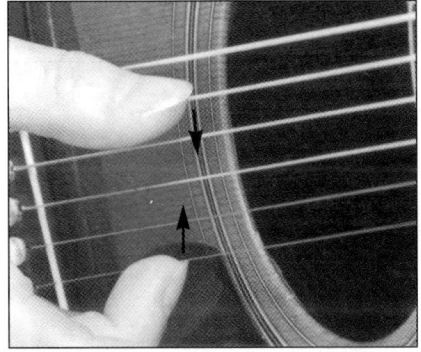

Picking the 5th and 1st strings with the thumb and middle finger.

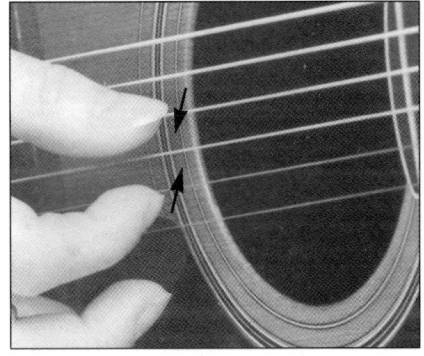

Picking the 4th and 2nd strings with the thumb and index finger.

At the same time as the thumb is plucking down on a bass string, you can pluck *up* on a treble string with your index or middle finger.

Practise this slowly at first, *remembering to keep an even beat.*

Fingerpicks

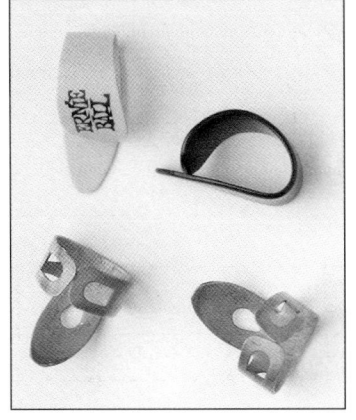

Some guitarists prefer picks instead of their nails. These are available made of plastic or metal. The best combination is a plastic thumb pick and two metal fingerpicks.

The fingerpicks are worn on the opposite side of the finger to the nail, that is, *not* like claws. *Note:* fingerpicks should only be used on steel strings.

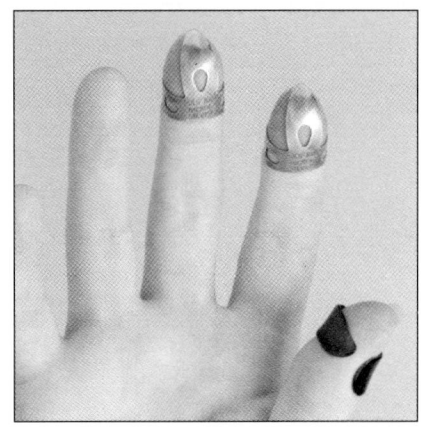

22 More about picking tunes

You won't always find the note you want in the chord you're fretting. If this is the case, then it's necessary to move your fingers around to pick out the tune. In the example shown here, the ④ above the stave means use your *left-hand 4th finger* to play the *1st string, 3rd fret*.

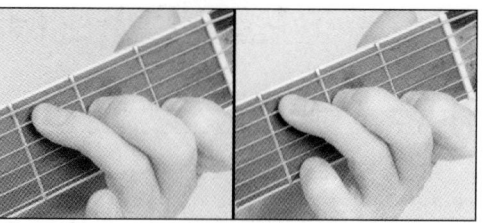
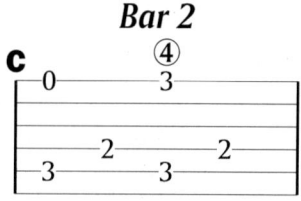

Bar 2

In this case, the ④ above the stave means use your *left-hand 4th finger* to play the *2nd string, 3rd fret*.

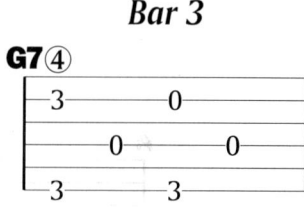

Bar 3

Skip to My Lou

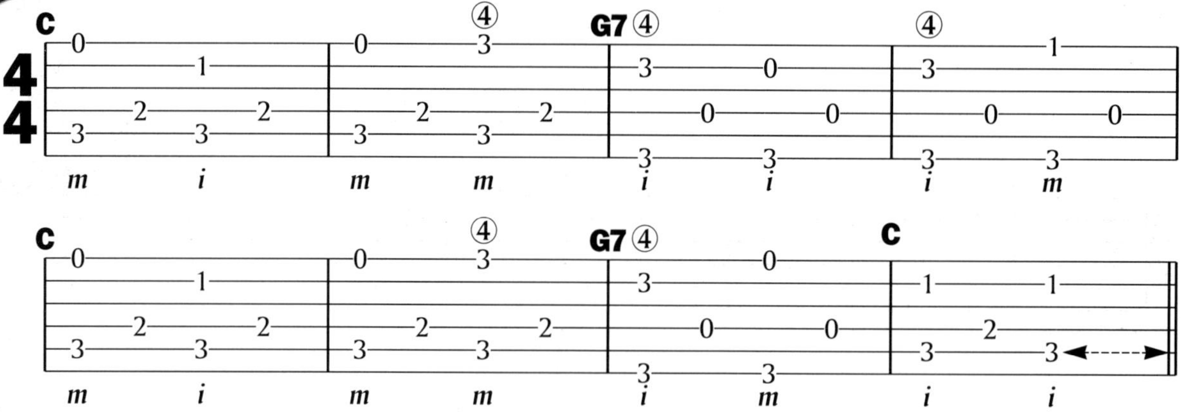

Track 24

Aunt Rhody

Track 25

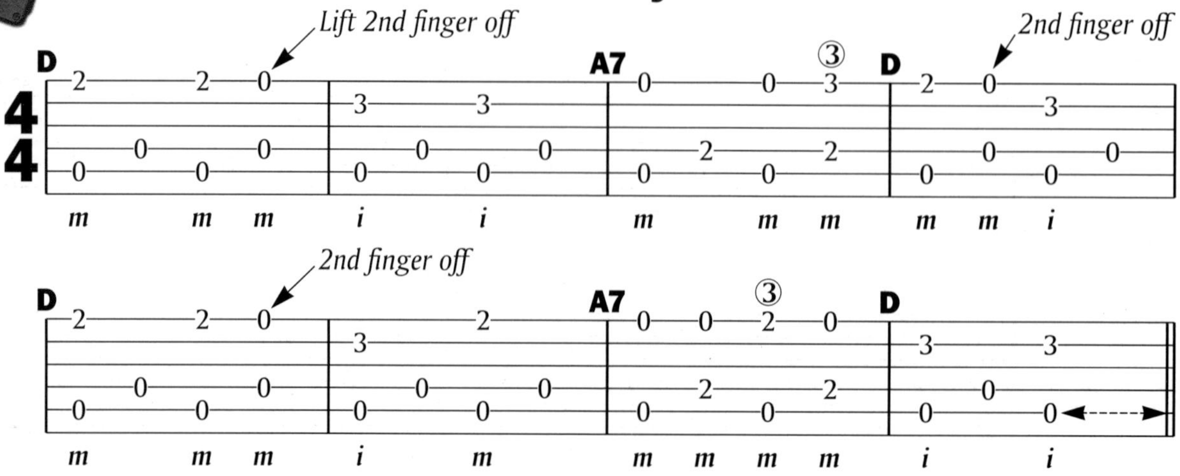

Pick Up The Guitar © Peter Flanagan & Dave Mallinson Publications 1997

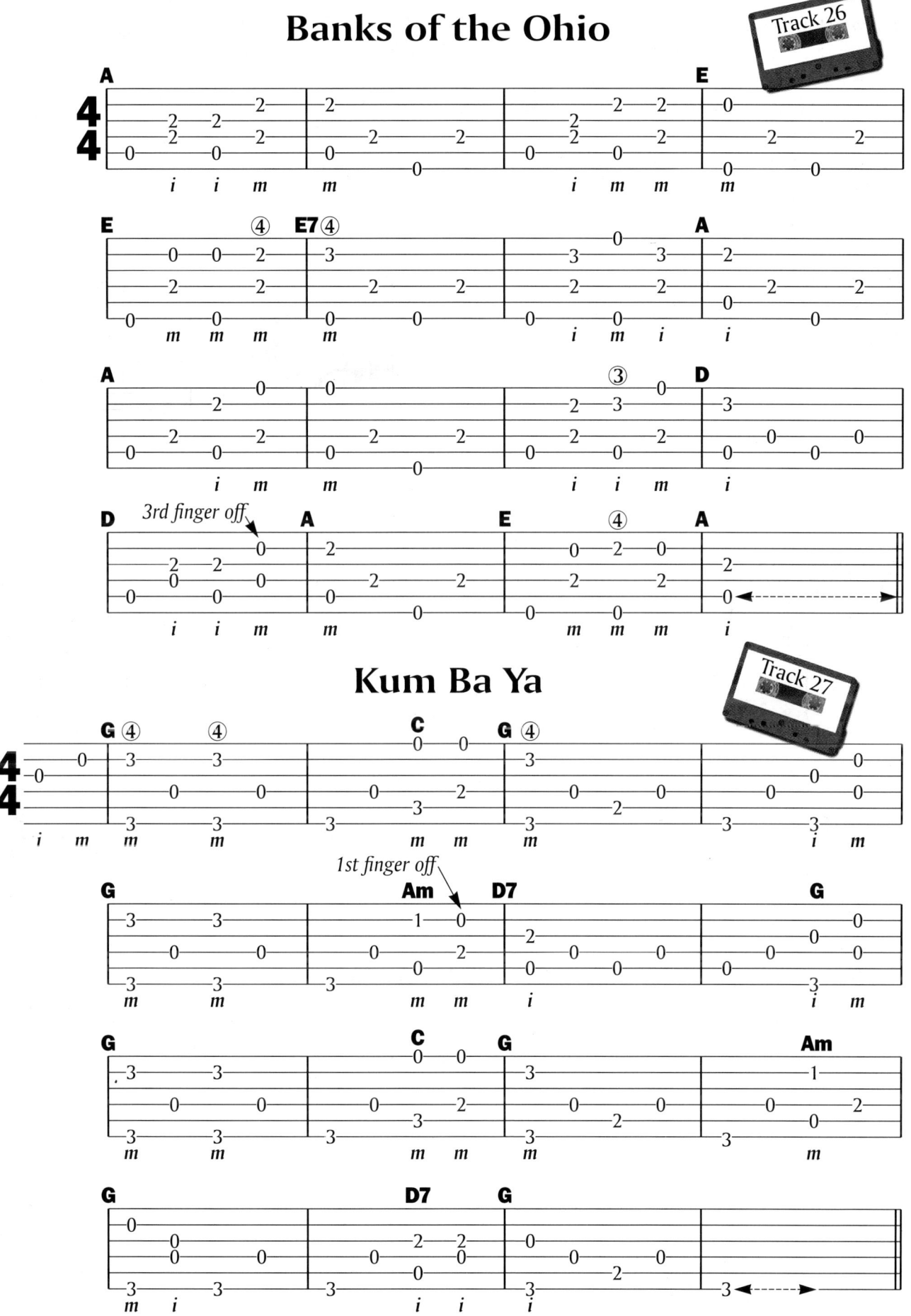

Maggie May

The Leaving of Liverpool

Grandfather's Clock *continued*

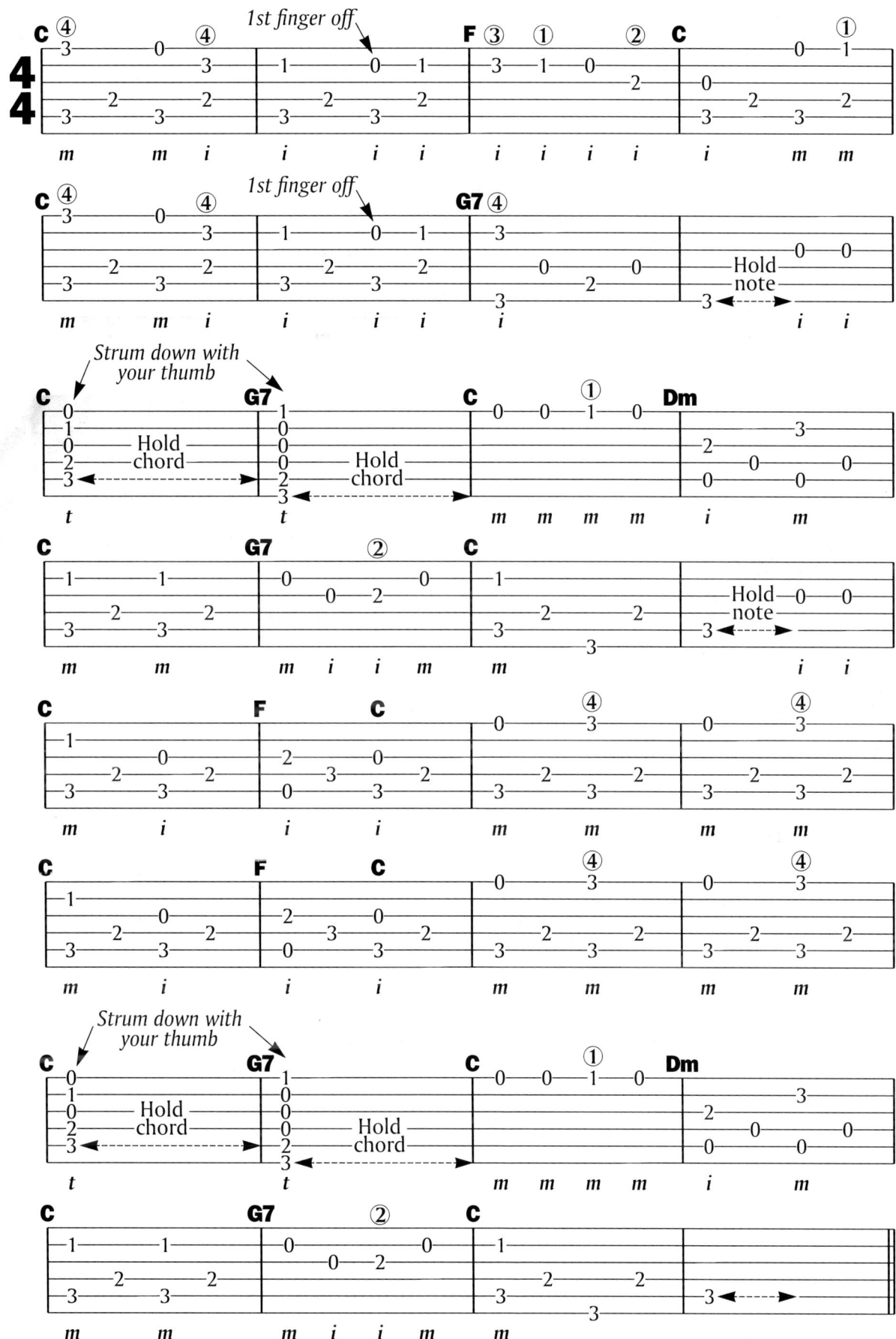

Picking off the beat

To make the tunes more interesting, some of the melody notes can be played *off* the beat. In other words, some notes can be played in between the steady bass accompaniment.

Practise the following *slowly* at first, remembering to keep an even beat with your thumb.

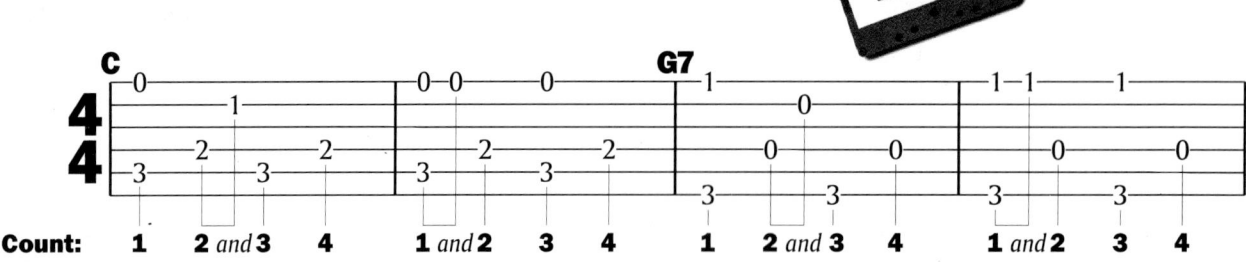

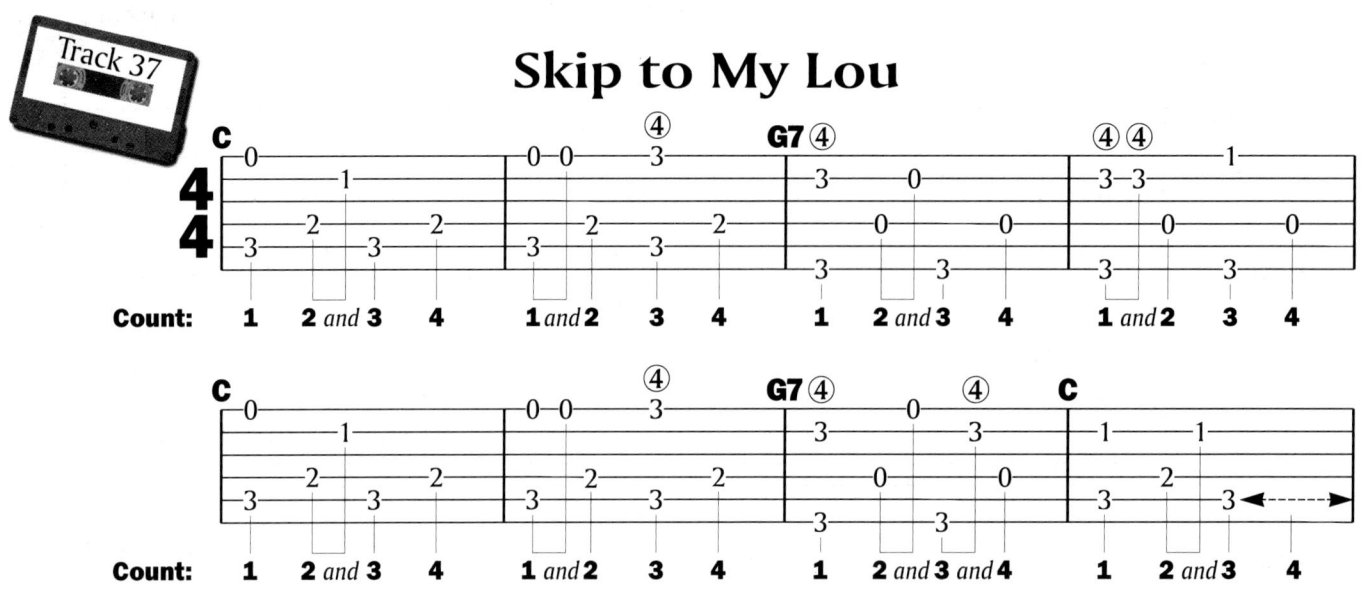

Skip to My Lou

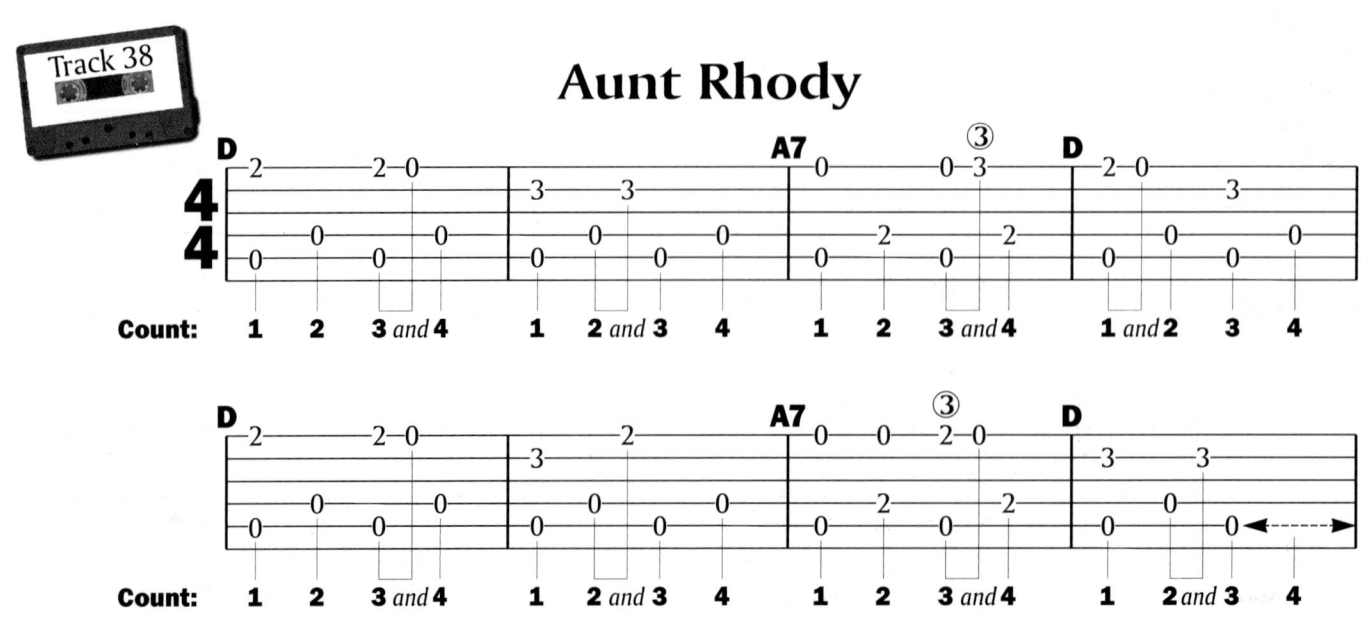

Aunt Rhody

Pick Up The Guitar © Peter Flanagan & Dave Mallinson Publications 1997

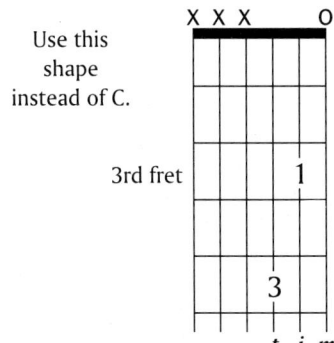

Use this shape instead of C.

3rd fret

In these last two pieces, use the shape on the left for the C chords. Make sure you use the correct right-hand fingering, which in this case is:

The *middle finger (m)* plays the 1st string;
The *index finger (i)* plays the 2nd string and
The *thumb (t)* plays the 3rd string.

Remember, these notes are played quickly (1 *and* 2 *and*).

Frère Jacques

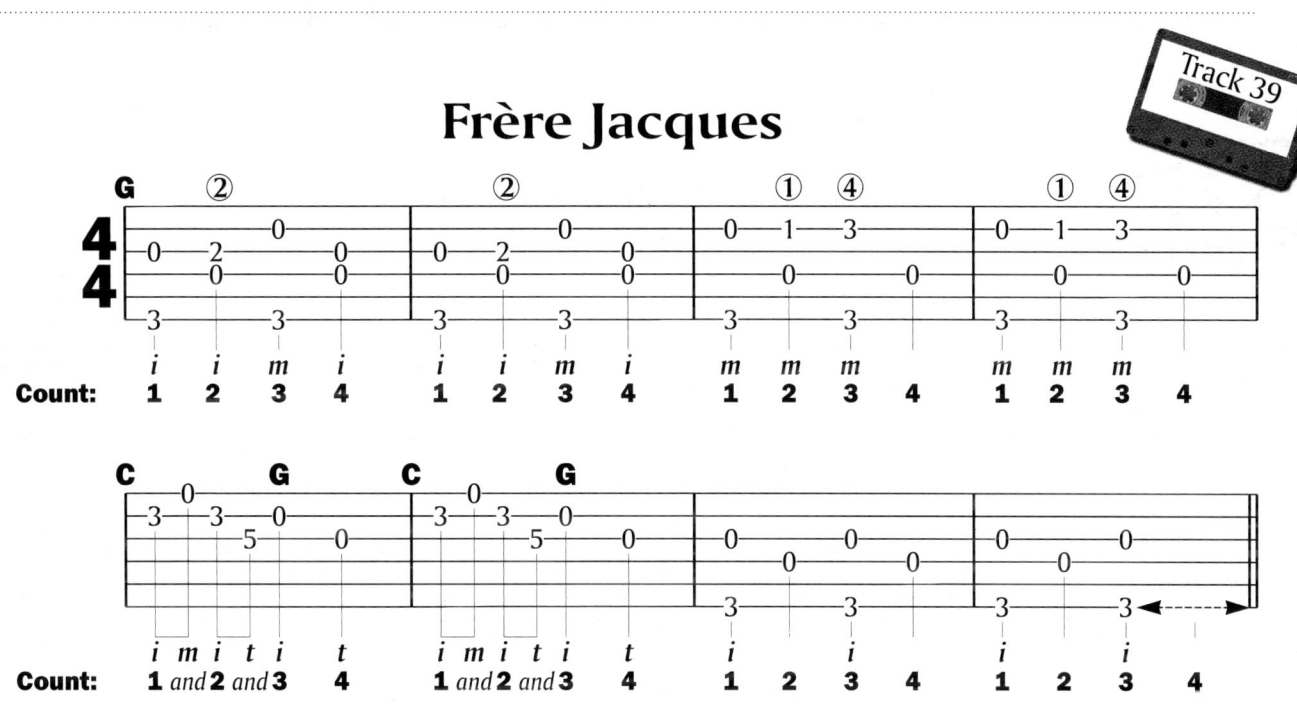

Coulter's Candy

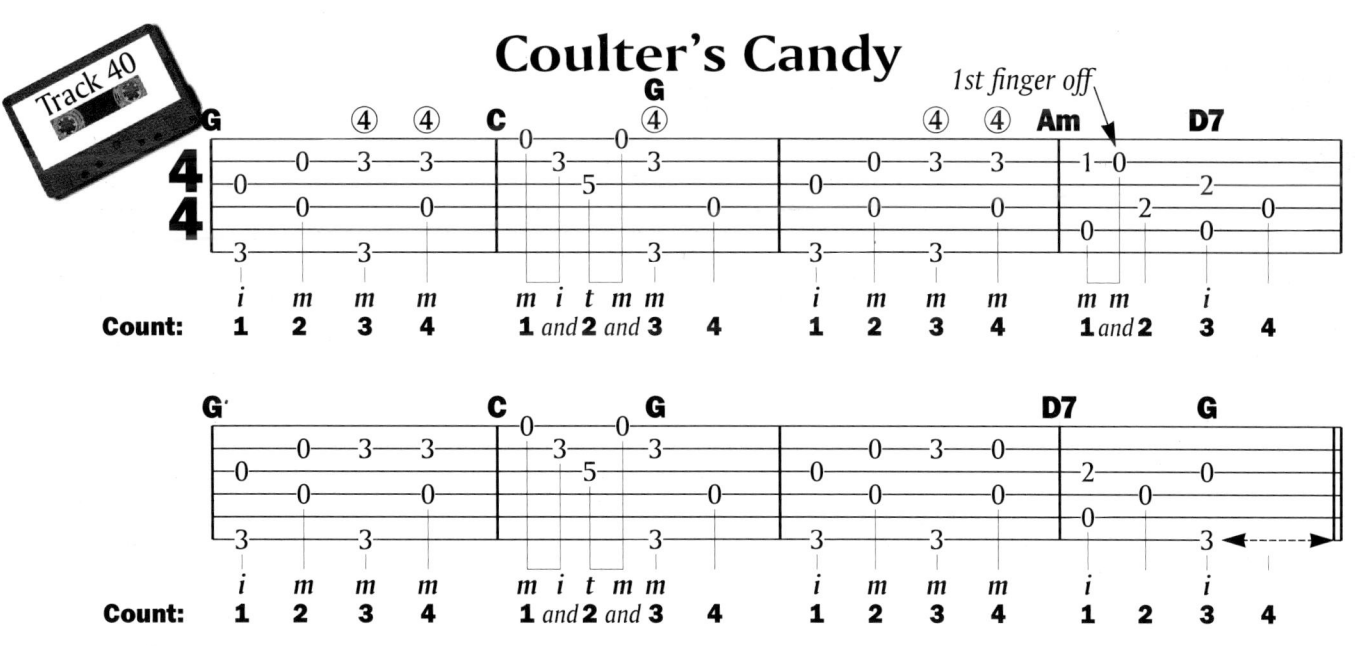

Pick Up The Guitar © Peter Flanagan & Dave Mallinson Publications 1997

The capo

The tunes in this book have been arranged in one of five *keys:* C, G, D, A and Am (A minor).

In this book, to find which key a particular tune is in, look at the last chord. If that chord is C, for instance, you can be certain that the tune is in the key of C.

If you wish to raise the *pitch* (or key) of a tune or song, you can use a *capo*. You may wish to do this if you find the guitar is too low to sing along to.

If you position the capo, say, behind the 3rd fret and play in the key of C, the tune will actually come out in the key of E♭ (E flat).

Types of capo

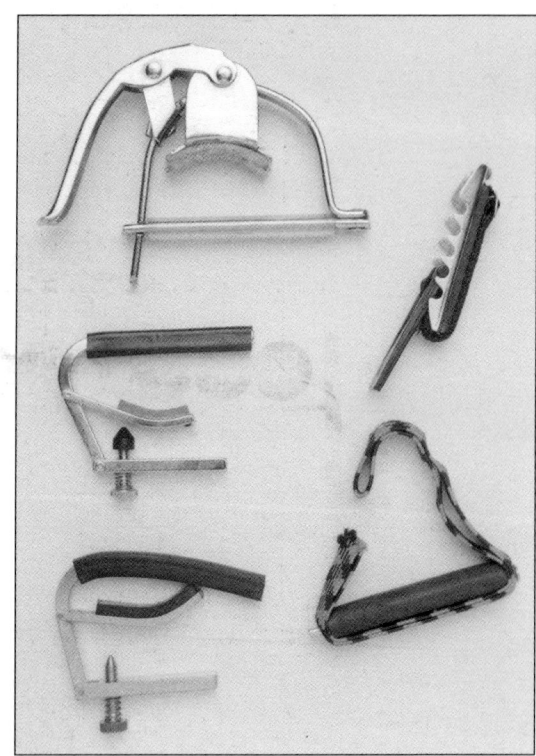

Capo position chart

	1st fret	2nd fret	3rd fret	4th fret	5th fret	6th fret	7th fret
Key of C	D♭ or C♯	D	E♭ or D♯	E	F	G♭ or F♯	G
Key of G	A♭ or G♯	A	B♭ or A♯	B	C	D♭ or C♯	D
Key of D	E♭ or D♯	E	F	G♭ or F♯	G	A♭ or G♯	A
Key of A	B♭ or A♯	B	C	D♭ or C♯	D	E♭ or D♯	E
Key of Am	B♭m or A♯m	Bm	Cm	D♭m or C♯m	Dm	E♭m or D♯m	Em

The sign ♯ is called a *sharp*.
The sign ♭ is called a *flat*.

Pick Up The Guitar © Peter Flanagan & Dave Mallinson Publications 1997